SURVIVAL IN
SPACE

The Apollo 13 Mission

DAVID LONG

Illustrated by
STEFANO TAMBELLINI

Barrington Stoke

*In memory of the victims of
Dora-Mittelbau and Peenemünde*

First published in 2020 in Great Britain by
Barrington Stoke Ltd
18 Walker Street, Edinburgh, EH3 7LP

www.barringtonstoke.co.uk

Text © 2020 David Long
Illustrations © 2020 Stefano Tambellini

A CIP catalogue record for this book is available
from the British Library upon request

ISBN: 978-1-78112-938-8

Printed by Hussar Books, Poland

Contents

1

THE RACE FOR SPACE

For hundreds of years men and women have gazed up at the Moon. Many have wanted to travel there, to find out what it is like. They thought their wish to take to the skies and fly was just an impossible dream. Some people tried to strap wings to their arms or made kites and colourful balloons to carry them up into the clouds.

The first real aeroplane was built by two American brothers called Orville and Wilbur Wright. It had flimsy wings of wood and cotton, and a small petrol engine. In 1903 their home-made machine flew for just 12 seconds before it came back down to earth with a bump. It had travelled less than 40 metres, but that was enough. The brothers had made history, and the age of powered flight had begun.

A few years later a Frenchman called Louis Blériot flew across the sea all the way to England, a distance of more than 20 miles. Soon bigger aircraft were built to carry passengers even longer distances, and more powerful jet engines meant humans could fly faster than any bird ever had. In the 1940s a bomber flew non-stop around the world, and in 1956 an English pilot called Peter Twiss became the first person to travel at more than 1,000 mph.

The public were excited about these daring record-breakers, and before long people began to think about travelling even further, maybe even out into space. Lots of rockets had been launched during the Second World War, but no one flew in them – they were just weapons, fired at the enemy. Once the war ended, people hoped the same technology could be used for science and exploration. Humans had spent so long looking up at the Moon, and now people began to dream that, one day, it might be possible to actually fly there ...

Scientists and engineers started to build bigger and more powerful rockets to travel out into space. Experts came from many different countries, but America and Russia led the way.

What became known as the Space Race really got going when the Russians launched their first satellite. This was called *Sputnik*, and shortly afterwards the Americans launched a rival satellite called the *Explorer 1*. The competition between the two countries got more and more intense as each tried to out-do the other.

In 1957 a Russian dog called Laika became
the first animal to orbit the Earth. Other
rockets carried rats and mice into space, as well
as frogs, flies, spiders, cats and chimpanzees.
Even tortoises and rabbits travelled on rockets,
but it took until 1961 before anyone dared to

send a human. The first man was Russia's
Yuri Gagarin, who spent a total of 108 minutes
in space. This was long enough for him to fly
right around our planet, which he said looked
beautiful from so far away. The first woman
in space was also Russian. She was called
Valentina Tereshkova and made her trip in 1963.

The Americans raced to catch up with Gagarin's great achievement. They did it less than a year later with a spacecraft so small that astronaut John Glenn couldn't even stand up inside it. He orbited the Earth three times in less than five hours, and shortly afterwards President John F. Kennedy made a famous

speech announcing that the Americans were planning a mission to the Moon. This news was incredibly exciting, but many scientists were worried about how long it would take to fly that far and how many billions of dollars it would cost.

In fact, the Americans had already sent rockets to the Moon, even before the president made his speech, but these didn't have anyone on board. Flying even an unmanned rocket all the way to the Moon was expensive and very difficult. Engineers knew that with a crew on board it would be much, much harder. In order to send a crew to the Moon they had to design a spaceship that could land safely and then bring the astronauts back home again afterwards. The president knew this too, but he was determined America was going to do it. He said the journey would be one of the greatest adventures of all time, and more than half a century later we can see that he was right.

2

THE LARGEST ROCKET EVER MADE

America called this great adventure the Apollo programme, and even now, more than 50 years later, it is reckoned to be the most complex and most expensive engineering project ever. Four hundred thousand men and women across America worked to make it happen. By the time it was over, a total of 24 astronauts had flown to the Moon. Twelve of them were lucky enough to stand on its surface and look back at Earth.

In order to make the longest journey in human history, they needed the largest and most powerful rockets ever made. The job of building these was given to an organisation called the National Aeronautics and Space Administration (NASA). Before the president had even finished his famous speech, NASA scientists and engineers were already working on a new rocket which they called the Saturn V.

This was designed to fly at more than 24,000 miles an hour. The rocket would take a small crew of three astronauts further from Earth than anyone had ever travelled before. It would also make it possible – for the first time in history – for humans to step off our world and onto another one.

The Saturn V was an astonishing machine.
A modern Formula One racing-car engine has
about 6,000 different parts, which sounds like a
lot until you compare it to the Saturn V rockets.
These needed more than 3 million components
to fly to the Moon and back. Each rocket
was 111 metres tall and weighed about the
same as 400 of the largest African elephants.
111 metres is taller than both the Statue of
Liberty in New York and Big Ben in London;
it's about the same height as a 35-storey office
block. In fact, the Saturn V rockets were so tall
that NASA's first job was to build a factory big
enough to fit them in.

The new factory was called the Vehicle
Assembly Building, and it is still one of the
most extraordinary buildings in the world.
Its roof is so high that rain clouds sometimes
form inside the building. The four main doors
are the biggest doors ever made. Each one
is 139 metres high and takes 45 minutes just
to open or close. Although the building is

much taller than many skyscrapers it has only a ground floor. This makes it the tallest single-storey building in the world. The space

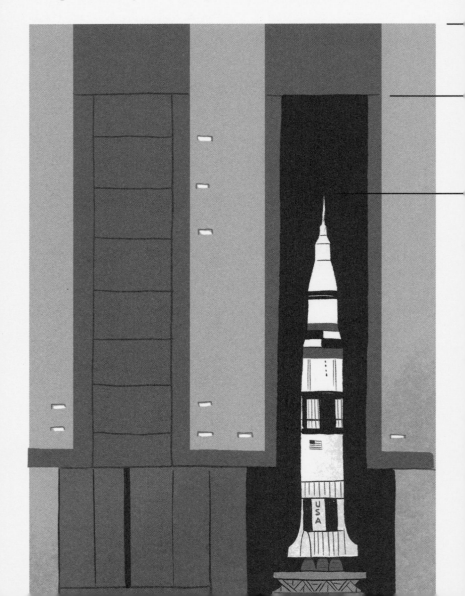

inside is so enormous that you could fit nearly 10,000 ordinary classrooms into it.

Vehicle Assembly Building   160m

Doors   139m

Saturn V   111m

Big Ben   96m

Statue of Liberty   93m

The Saturn V had to be big because it needed really powerful motors and these burn huge amounts of fuel. Almost all of this enormous machine was taken up by eleven powerful motors as well as gigantic tanks holding enough fuel to take off and fly more than half a million miles.

The five largest of those eleven motors are still the most powerful rocket motors ever made. Together they produce a total of 160 million horsepower. That's an extraordinary amount of power, especially when you compare it to other high-speed machines that were being built at this time. Ferrari's most popular sports car, for example, was called the Dino. It was one of the fastest cars in the world, but its engine produced less than 200 horsepower.

The Saturn V needed all this power just to escape the Earth's gravity, and the amount of fuel needed to produce that power was enormous. Instead of petrol or diesel, these huge new rockets used an expensive and highly explosive mix of kerosene, hydrogen and oxygen. The five largest motors burned most of it just taking off. In fact, the Saturn V used more fuel in one second than the first plane to fly across the Atlantic Ocean needed to fly 3,600 miles in $33^1/_2$ hours.

NASA built Saturn Vs in huge sections. The sections were known as "stages", and each one had its own supply of fuel. The stages were the parts of the rocket that powered it, but there was no room for the astronauts among all the engines.

The three-man crew was squeezed into a small cone-shaped capsule at the very tip of the rocket. This was called the Command Module, and it was the only bit of the rocket that was designed to come back to Earth. The Command Module wasn't much bigger than a garden shed, so it was very cramped and uncomfortable.

Below the Command Module were the Service Module and the Lunar Module. The Service Module held more motors, and the Lunar Module was the part of the spaceship that the astronauts used to land on the Moon.

The other sections, which held mostly fuel, were much, much larger. The bottom stage was easily the biggest. It was fitted with the five most powerful motors because it was designed for the hardest task of all. This was lifting the whole 2,900-tonne rocket off the ground.

STAGE 1 with five large F-1 engines

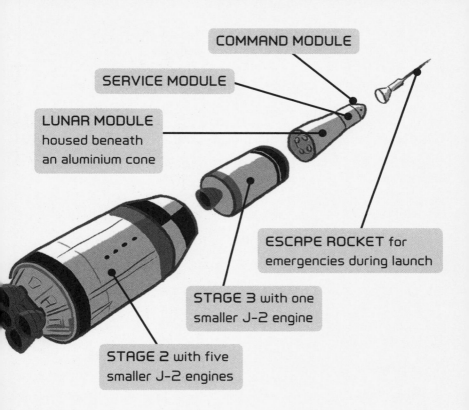

COMMAND MODULE

SERVICE MODULE

LUNAR MODULE housed beneath an aluminium cone

ESCAPE ROCKET for emergencies during launch

STAGE 3 with one smaller J-2 engine

STAGE 2 with five smaller J-2 engines

Once it had done this, the bottom stage was no longer needed. It separated from the rocket and splashed down into the sea. The middle stage then took the crew almost into orbit around the Earth before it too ran out of fuel and was discarded. Finally, the third stage propelled the astronauts on towards the Moon before then also being disconnected.

The first stage is jettisoned less than 3 minutes after the launch.

The second stage is jettisoned approximately 6 minutes later.

The crew in the Command Module turn it around to link up with the Lunar Module.

Both parts travel to the moon, but only the Lunar Module will land on its surface.

All this happened incredibly quickly once a rocket was launched. Millions of litres of fuel were burned up in just a few minutes. The first stage contained approximately 2,000 tonnes of fuel, but this was all gone before the rocket had even climbed 50 miles into the sky. This much fuel would be enough for an ordinary family car to drive more than 20 million miles. The second stage contained only 450 tonnes of fuel, but even this would be enough to refuel all 21,000 of London's famous black taxis.

With so much highly inflammable fuel and so many tiny components, there was a lot which could go wrong with a Saturn V rocket. Various practice launches were made without anybody on board. These were spectacular and exciting but incredibly dangerous. Thousands of people waited for hours to watch, but they had to stand at least three miles away in case a rocket exploded. Luckily this never happened, but three astronauts were killed when the first Saturn V with a crew on board caught fire before it had even left the ground in a test launch on 27 January 1967.

It wasn't just the launches which could be dangerous. Everyone at NASA knew that everything about space travel is difficult and dangerous. It's one of the reasons that only a few people have ever been to the Moon. After the terrible fire in 1967, it took more than two years of testing and retesting the Saturn V – manned and unmanned – before a new crew was finally given permission to attempt to fly to the Moon and land on its surface.

3

WE HAVE LIFT-OFF!

The details of this new mission sounded almost unbelievable, and the excitement around the world was incredible. Russia's heroic Yuri Gagarin had flown just over 200 miles into space when he became the first man to orbit the Earth. Now a three-man crew was planning to fly a Saturn V rocket, the *Apollo 11*, more than half a million miles. If everything went to plan, Neil Armstrong, Buzz Aldrin and Michael Collins would spend longer in space than anyone had ever done before: a total of eight days, three hours, 18 minutes and 35 seconds.

Even more amazing was the fact that two of them were going to try to walk on the Moon. Armstrong and Aldrin had been chosen by NASA to fly down to the rocky surface in the Lunar Module. This was codenamed "Eagle" and only had room inside for two men. Collins would have to stay in the Command Module and continue flying around the Moon approximately 60 miles above their heads.

It was the first time anything like this had been attempted, and on the morning of 16 July 1969 millions of people around the world turned on their televisions to see the three men climbing into the tiny capsule at the top of the rocket. Another million travelled to Cape Canaveral in Florida to see the launch for themselves. Some were VIPs who had been invited to sit in special grandstands a safe distance away from the launchpad, but most were ordinary men, women and children who crowded into little boats and onto the sandy beaches nearby to watch as the countdown began.

When the countdown finally reached zero, the sound of the *Apollo 11*'s first five rocket motors firing up was deafening. A roar like rolling thunder caused buildings in the area to tremble, and the ground seemed to shake as the astronauts' historic journey finally got underway. A great wall of fire shot from the base of the rocket, and as it lifted off the launchpad massive clouds of thick smoke rose into the air.

The noise inside the capsule was even more terrifying, and the whole rocket shook

violently from the release of energy needed to propel the heavy machine into the sky. For several seconds the huge G-forces caused by the rocket's acceleration made it almost impossible for the men inside to move their arms or legs.

In less than five minutes the rocket was flying as high as a passenger jet. After 12 minutes, Armstrong, Aldrin and Collins were travelling at more than 20,000 miles an hour. Despite travelling at such a high speed, it would still take the crew of *Apollo 11* four days to even get close to the Moon.

Because it was such a long journey the crew needed to eat plenty of meals. These came in small plastic bags. All the meals were freeze-dried, so before they could eat them, the astronauts had to inject warm water into each bag. Then they simply squeezed the contents of the bag into their mouths. What came out didn't look much like real food, but it tasted of beef or biscuits or bacon with apple sauce.

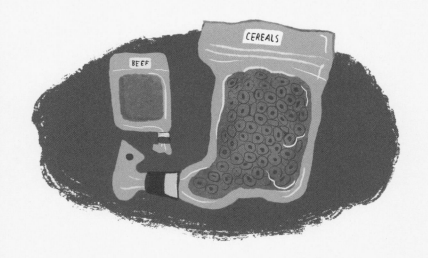

The Command Module was fitted with five small windows made of thick pieces of special glass. When they looked outside, the crew could see the Earth getting smaller and smaller as they flew further and further away. Before long our whole world appeared to be no larger than a glass marble, a bright blue-green dot set against the endless black sky. It was still possible for the men to talk to Mission Control, which was based at Houston in Texas, but now it took several seconds for even the shortest radio messages to travel thousands of miles from the spaceship back to Earth.

There was no gravity in space, so everything floated around the capsule unless it was tied down or fixed to something. The men's sleeping bags had to be strapped to the walls, and everyone slept standing up. Zero gravity also made going to the toilet very awkward. It involved more plastic bags and short hosepipes, but this is something most astronauts don't like talking about!

After the crew finally entered the Moon's orbit on the fourth day of the mission, it was time for Armstrong and Aldrin to start putting on their spacesuits and helmets. This was something else which was hard to do in such a cramped space. Without any gravity the suits weren't heavy, but they were extremely stiff. This made it difficult to put them on and to move around. Also it was really hard for Armstrong and Aldrin to crawl out of the capsule and into the Lunar Module.

The suits were stiff because they were made of lots of different layers of material to protect the men from dangerous cosmic radiation and from the heat and cold on the Moon. The glare of the sun means temperatures on the surface of the Moon can reach well over boiling point. In the shade temperatures fall to -153°C. The men's eyes also needed protecting from the sun, so the visors of their helmets were covered in a very thin layer of pure gold.

Once the men were inside the Lunar Module, this separated from the capsule and began its short journey down to the Moon. A couple of hours later, Armstrong sent a brief radio message back to Mission Control announcing that "the Eagle has landed". Armstrong and Aldrin were on the surface of the Moon! It was now clear that America had won the Space Race. After looking up at the night sky for thousands of years, humans had finally landed on the Moon.

None of the astronauts knew it yet, but back on Earth more than half a billion people were staring at their television screens. Millions of viewers in different countries all over the world wanted to witness NASA's exciting adventure as it happened. Of course what people wanted to see most of all was someone actually walking on the Moon. When first Armstrong and then Aldrin left the Lunar Module and climbed down a short ladder to the ground, they were being watched by the largest television audience in the whole of the 20th century.

4

UNLUCKY THIRTEEN

When Neil Armstrong first set foot on the Moon, he said it was "one small step for a man, one giant leap for Mankind". This was his clever way of saying that the *Apollo 11* mission was not just an important achievement for him but an important achievement for all of us. He and Aldrin spent less than three hours walking on the surface, but just by being there the American astronauts had made history. When the crew got back to Earth a few days later, all three were welcomed as heroes.

Having shown that it was possible to fly from this world to another one, NASA was determined to do it again, and there was another successful moon landing a few months later. But ordinary people weren't as interested as they had been the first time. Fewer people went to watch the *Apollo 12* launch, and television audiences were much, much smaller than they had been before. It is hard to think that people were already bored by space travel, but it was only when the next mission went badly wrong that the public really got interested again.

In April 1970, another rocket was ready to take off from Cape Canaveral. *Apollo 13*'s mission commander was Jim Lovell. He was a highly experienced pilot who had already made three trips into space, including the first manned flight right around the Moon. His two crewmates were Jack Swigert and Fred Haise.

The launch of *Apollo 13* went well. The giant first and second stages of the rocket were successfully discarded, and three hours later the third stage was jettisoned too. The crew settled down inside the little Command Module as it raced towards the Moon at thousands of miles an hour.

Everything was going according to plan, and at Mission Control in Houston someone even said that things were looking a bit boring. Then suddenly, on the third day, something terrible happened that changed everything.

Without any warning a broken electrical wire had made a tiny spark in the Service Module. The spark caused a fire, and then an explosion ripped apart one oxygen tank and badly damaged another. The spaceship shook dangerously, and radio communication with Mission Control was suddenly cut off.

Luckily it took only a few seconds to fix the radio, but now several warning lights were flashing in the Command Module. The explosion had made a huge hole in one of the oxygen tanks, and the gas inside it was leaking out fast. When Jim Lovell looked out of the window, he saw the jet of oxygen shooting out into space, but he knew there was nothing the crew could do to plug the hole or to stop the oxygen escaping.

One of the other astronauts, Jack Swigert, quickly sent a radio message to Mission Control: "Houston, we've had a problem." He and Lovell and Haise still had enough air to breathe, but losing so much oxygen in this way could be catastrophic.

When the explosion happened, *Apollo 13* was more than 200,000 miles from Earth. This meant the men were much closer to the Moon than the Earth, but all three knew at once that they wouldn't be able to complete their mission. This was disappointing but also incredibly frightening. It was disappointing because the crew had been training for months. It was frightening because the damage from the explosion might make it impossible for them to fly back home to Earth.

The oxygen in the tanks was meant to power the rocket's three fuel cells. The fuel cells were needed to generate electricity and for making water. Both of these were vital for the crew's survival, but now two of the cells wouldn't work. Almost everything in the spaceship ran on electricity, and of course the crew had to have drinking water. Humans can survive for days or even weeks without food, but no one can last very long without a drink.

There was nothing anyone could do to get the lost oxygen back into the tanks or to get the fuel cells working again. It was a desperate situation.

5

SURVIVAL STATIONS

When Swigert sent his emergency SOS message to Mission Control, he sounded calm. The flight controller in Houston sounded just as calm when he asked Lovell to repeat what Swigert had just said, but everyone knew that the three men were now in big trouble.

The explosion on *Apollo 13* was a horrible reminder to scientists and the public about how difficult and dangerous space missions are. Suddenly nobody was bored by space travel any more – the whole world was watching as these three men tried to find a way home.

NASA's Apollo crews spent a lot of time training before each launch. One of the reasons they did this was so they would know what to

do if something went wrong. In a complicated
machine like the Saturn V there's a lot that can
go wrong, and everyone involved in the Apollo
programme knew that even if something small
breaks, it can easily turn into a disaster. This
looked like one of those occasions. A faulty
wire is only a small thing to go wrong, but an

explosion on a spaceship is a disaster when it happens more than 200,000 miles from base.

The problems the three men now faced were not ones anyone could have expected, not even a commander like Lovell, who was NASA's most experienced astronaut. Luckily many months of training helped him and his crew to make some smart decisions in the first few moments after the incident.

No one knew yet how to get them home, or if it would be possible to do this. However, the crew guessed that even if it was possible, it would take many hours or even days for Mission Control to come up with a rescue plan that might work. While the flight controllers down on Earth were busy trying to think of a plan to save them, Lovell, Swigert and Haise knew they had to preserve as much of their air and power as they could. The only way to do this was to use as little oxygen and electricity as possible.

Because the Command Module was the only part of the rocket designed to come back to Earth, it made sense not to use up its air supply or power. The crew decided to climb into the Lunar Module while they waited for instructions from Mission Control. If they stayed in this for as long as possible, using it as a sort of emergency lifeboat, the Command Module's oxygen and power could be saved. That way there might be enough of both to get the three of them home safely.

This sounded like a good idea, but there was a problem. The Command Module was small inside, but it had been designed to fit all three astronauts on a journey of more than 500,000 miles. The Lunar Module was designed for only two of them. It was also meant for a much shorter journey, one of only about 60 miles down to the Moon's surface and then another 60 back up into orbit. On a normal mission two astronauts share the Lunar Module for only a day and a half. Now it looked as though all three of them would have to spend at least four days in it.

Four days was how long the people at Mission Control thought it would take the astronauts to fly back home. But so far no one had worked out a way for them to do this.

6

MISSION CONTROL

While the astronauts were doing everything they could to save air and electricity, hundreds of engineers and technicians back on Earth were looking for other ways to help them. To begin with they told the astronauts which pieces of equipment on the spacecraft they

could safely switch off and which pieces had to be kept on. This was helpful, but Lovell, Swigert and Haise had a much bigger problem, and everyone at Mission Control knew they didn't have much time to solve it.

Apollo 13 had been heading away from Earth when the explosion occurred. After the explosion, it was still travelling towards the Moon, and it was still doing this at thousands of miles an hour. In space, even without any power, an object will keep going until it hits something. As there is no air in space, there isn't any friction to slow it down. Because of this, *Apollo 13* kept moving in roughly the same direction and at roughly the same speed as it had been doing before the explosion. In other words, as each minute passed, the three men were getting further and further from home.

You might think the easiest thing would be for them to just turn the rocket around and fly back to Earth, but things are never that simple when you're this far out in space.

The three main stages of the rocket had been jettisoned, so *Apollo 13* now had only one small rocket motor left and hardly any fuel. Turning around would use up a lot of that fuel, so NASA engineers knew that wasn't the right thing to do. They believed the crew's only hope of survival was to keep travelling towards the Moon and then to fly around the Moon before changing course for Earth. This sounds complicated, and it is. Nothing like it had ever been tried before, and even the smartest people at NASA couldn't be sure if it would work.

The maths involved in working out a solution was incredibly complicated, and of course every calculation had to be 100 per cent accurate. For the mathematicians this was

another reminder of how even something small going wrong can lead to a disaster. Even a tiny error in one of their calculations, a single careless sum, could lead to the deaths of three brave men. To make matters worse, all the calculations had to be done as quickly as possible. The men on *Apollo 13* were running out of air, running out of electricity – and running out of time. Calculations about fuel, speed and direction would normally take months to do properly – now they had to be completed in days or even hours.

At this point nobody thought *Apollo 13* was boring. Finding the right answers was urgent and exhausting work for everyone on the ground, but it was also exciting. Millions of ordinary people were desperate for news as the three astronauts battled for survival, helped by hundreds of scientists at NASA. For days and nights no one at NASA went home to eat or sleep. If anyone needed a break, he or she lay on the floor beneath a desk for a few hours and then got back to work. It wasn't very comfortable, but it was a lot better than the conditions on board *Apollo 13*.

Up there, hundreds of thousands of miles away, the conditions inside the "lifeboat" were getting worse. The astronauts had switched off the lights and main computer to save power, and the Lunar Module was soon cold and damp. Outside, the temperature was about

270° below freezing, which no one can survive. The Lunar Module wasn't that cold inside, but it was getting colder as each hour passed. Before long it was nearly freezing, which made it almost impossible to get any sleep, and the men had to hug each other just to stay warm. They didn't mind this – they could all cope with some discomfort. But with three of them on board a spacecraft designed for two, the air inside was turning poisonous ...

7

STICKY TAPE AND SOCKS

Humans breathe in oxygen and breathe out a gas called carbon dioxide. Normally this isn't a problem. The gas you breathe out usually drifts away, but in an enclosed space it can quickly build up and reach dangerous levels. It doesn't smell, so it can do this without anyone noticing.

Because of this it is sometimes called "the silent killer".

In a car full of people breathing out carbon dioxide the driver can just open a window. In a spacecraft this isn't possible, so astronauts have to rely on devices called "scrubbers". These use chemicals to filter out the poisonous carbon dioxide. When the chemicals get used up, the scrubber has to be replaced.

Sitting in the cold and dark, the astronauts couldn't smell anything, and so far no one was having difficulty breathing. However, they knew that with three of them in a small space the level of carbon dioxide gas inside the Lunar Module was going up. They knew that in the end it would start to poison them.

Luckily the Lunar Module was fitted with scrubbers. But they were designed to keep two astronauts alive for 36 hours and not three of them for 96 hours. The scrubbers would stop working sooner than they were meant to. The Lunar Module didn't have any replacement scrubbers because on a normal mission no one stayed in it for very long.

Soon the scrubbers did begin to fail, and the amount of carbon dioxide started to increase. Mission Control was worried about the gas and advised the men to climb back into the Command Module and borrow some of the scrubbers in there. The astronauts found the new scrubbers, but they were the wrong shape. The ones inside the Lunar Module were round; those inside the Command Module were square. This meant they wouldn't fit.

The flight controllers knew that if something wasn't done quickly the crew would get sick and die. Then someone at NASA had a bright idea. A small team of engineers shut themselves in a room and started to try out different bits of equipment to see if they could find a way to attach the square scrubbers to

the circular plugs in the Lunar Module. They needed to find a simple solution, one the astronauts could copy in a hurry. They could only use bits of equipment which the astronauts already had up in the spacecraft. If they could do it fast enough, the astronauts would be able to breathe clean oxygen again. If they couldn't, the mission would end in tragedy.

Racing against the clock, they eventually found a way to make the square scrubbers fit the round holes. It was a brilliant solution but also quite a funny one because the engineers could only do it by using all sorts of weird stuff to fit the square filters in place. This included bits of spacesuit, plastic bags, ordinary sticky tape and even a pair of the astronauts' socks.

As soon as the engineers had worked out how to fit everything together, Mission Control radioed the crew to tell them what they had done. They then read out clear instructions so the astronauts could copy the engineers. The result looked a real mess, and it didn't look like it would work for very long. But the main thing was that it worked. The new scrubbers helped reduce the carbon dioxide to a safe level and kept the crew alive in their increasingly cold and uncomfortable lifeboat.

8

HEADING FOR HOME

At the start of the mission, *Apollo 13* had the Saturn V's eleven powerful rocket motors and thousands of tonnes of fuel. Now Lovell, Swigert and Haise were left with only the Lunar Module's landing rocket motor and almost no fuel.

After the explosion, the flight controllers at Mission Control calculated that the astronauts would have the best possible chance of survival if they continued flying towards the Moon. *Apollo 13* was much too damaged to land on the

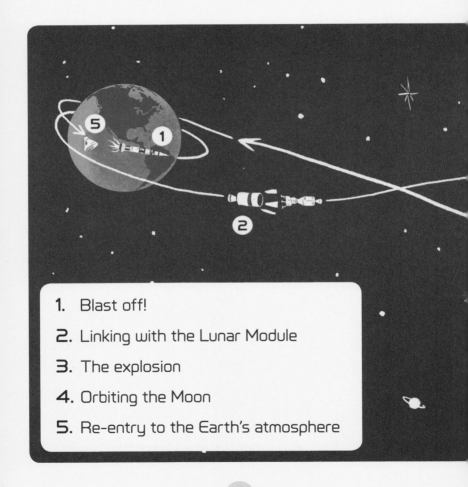

1. Blast off!
2. Linking with the Lunar Module
3. The explosion
4. Orbiting the Moon
5. Re-entry to the Earth's atmosphere

Moon, so the crew were told to fly thousands of miles round it. After going around the Moon, the rocket would be pointing back towards Earth, and it might be possible to get the crew home.

The idea of travelling even further away must have been terrifying, and no one at NASA could be entirely sure that it would work. Everyone hoped the remaining fuel would be enough to power the last rocket motor so that it could be fired for a few short bursts to move the damaged spacecraft into the correct position. One burst would pull the spacecraft out of its orbit around the Moon and put it on the right path back to Earth. Another burst of power would be needed to pull the spacecraft out of its orbit around the Earth and into the Earth's atmosphere so that the crew could reach safety.

The rocket had to be fired in precisely the right way and for exactly the right amount of time. Normally this would be done automatically, by computer, but the spacecraft's computer systems had been switched off to save electricity. Now the men had to do it themselves, using the sun to help them navigate. It was going to be very hard work, and it needed their total concentration. Lovell, Swigert and Haise would all die in space if any of the fuel was wasted. To make matters worse, all three were beginning to lose weight due to a lack of food. Also their water was now running out, and Fred Haise had developed an infection.

Despite all this the crew worked to get it right. At last they fired the short burst needed to get the spacecraft into the right position.

They used the complicated calculations made by the mathematicians at NASA and were soon on their way back to Earth. Now there was even less fuel. All that was left were the last few drops needed to fire up the rocket one last time. If it worked, the spacecraft would move out of orbit and be able to fly down for the last part of its journey through the Earth's atmosphere.

The Lunar Module was designed to land on the Moon, so it could not be used for this final stage. The crew had to climb back into the Command Module, which was the only part of the spacecraft with a heatshield. The shield was needed to protect the crew from the enormous heat of re-entry into the Earth's atmosphere.

Inside the Command Module it was as cold and dark as the Lunar Module. The walls were dripping with condensation because the heating had been switched off to save power. The crew had very little time to switch everything back on and couldn't be sure the computer systems would work because of the damp. Luckily they managed to get everything running again before jettisoning the damaged Service Module. They were now able to fire the rocket for a final time and then jettison the Lunar Module in preparation for re-entry, but they still weren't safe.

As *Apollo 13* entered the final stage of its journey, all anyone could do was hope and pray.

9

SPLASHDOWN!

The effects of the explosion were nerve-wracking for the crew and for everyone at Mission Control, but the final stage of *Apollo 13*'s long journey was perhaps the worst of all. Incredibly, Lovell, Swigert and Haise had managed to fly their damaged spacecraft all the way to the Moon and back, but there was still a very real chance that they would be killed in the last few minutes.

When a spacecraft re-enters the Earth's atmosphere, it is travelling at nearly seven miles a second. The enormous heat which builds up around the capsule due to friction makes this one of the most dangerous parts of any mission. If everything goes well, three parachutes eventually open to slow the capsule down, and it splashes down safely into the sea. But even a tiny amount of damage to the heatshield can be catastrophic, and more astronauts have been killed during their re-entry than have ever died in space.

Crews lose radio contact with Mission Control for several minutes when their capsules re-enter the Earth's atmosphere. This is called a blackout and it is perfectly normal. But with no radio contact, no one at Mission Control knows what is going on during this very

dangerous stage, and if the astronauts have a
problem none of the flight controllers can help
them. Re-entry is an extremely tense time for
everyone, especially while the spacecraft is too
high and moving much too fast for anyone to
see it from the ground.

Worries about *Apollo 13*'s parachutes and heatshield meant everyone was even more nervous this time. With no radio it was impossible to know if the three men were still alive or if their capsule had exploded. To make matters worse, the blackout lasted longer than usual, around six minutes instead of four or five. But then, finally, a tiny speck was spotted high above the South Pacific. As the silvery shape grew larger and clearer, it soon became obvious it was *Apollo 13*.

The heatshield had done its job and saved the capsule, but there was still no sign of the parachutes. People watched and waited. Hundreds of eyes strained to see into the bright blue sky. For a time there was nothing, and then, suddenly, three huge red and white shapes billowed out of the top of the capsule. All three of the parachutes had worked! Moments later *Apollo 13* and its heroic crew splashed down into the sea.

Within three minutes of the capsule hitting the water, rescue helicopters arrived on the scene. The three astronauts were quickly flown to a nearby US Navy vessel, the *Iwo Jima*. They spent the night on board the ship before they were flown to the island of Samoa, where their families were all waiting for them.

Against all odds, Lovell, Swigert and Haise were home and they were safe.

10

THE LONGEST JOURNEY

You could say that *Apollo 13* was a failure because the mission's aim was for another two astronauts to walk on the Moon, and no one got there. But in another sense, a more important sense, it turned out to be a spectacular success.

For nearly four days the lives of three astronauts had hung in the balance. The explosion put Lovell, Swigert and Haise in terrible danger. They were hundreds of thousands of miles from home, they were heading in the wrong direction, and no one could fix their damaged spacecraft. The fact that all three managed to get back alive turned what looked like a disaster into one of the greatest survival stories of all time.

The mission was remarkable in other ways too. Almost half a century after *Apollo 13*'s capsule splashed down safely into the Pacific Ocean, Lovell, Swigert and Haise still hold an important record. The three men travelled further from Earth than any human had managed to do before, and still no one has beaten them. When their "lifeboat" passed round the far side of the Moon, the three Americans were an astonishing 248,655 miles from home.

In fact, in just under six days the crew of *Apollo 13* flew a total of more than 622,268 miles, or about the same as driving around the world almost 25 times. This would have been an amazing achievement for a healthy crew in a working spacecraft. For three exhausted guys in a broken one it's almost unbelievable, especially in freezing conditions without enough light, food and water.

It's true these men never got to land on the Moon, and that must have been a terrible disappointment for them and for everyone else at NASA. But the *Apollo 13* story is still a positive one, and not just because they all survived.

Lovell, Swigert and Haise stayed calm when most ordinary people would have panicked, and they showed true bravery in the face of danger. That got them through the worst of it, but they were also lucky. Lucky that the capsule's heatshield didn't fail. Lucky that their parachutes still worked. And lucky that the water dripping down the walls of the capsule didn't stop the electrical systems working when they left the Lunar Module and returned to the Command Module.

But mostly Lovell, Swigert and Haise were lucky to have a great team at NASA. Their bravery was hugely impressive, but so was the quick thinking and hard work of NASA's engineers. No one else could have fixed the poisonous gas problem, or done it as fast. The mathematicians were the ones who helped work out if the astronauts could pull their crippled spacecraft out of orbit and get it back on course to Earth.

Really that's what makes the *Apollo 13* mission such a great story. It shows us that people can often achieve far more than they think they can, especially when they work together.